INSTANT POT COOKBOOK

*Eating Healthy and Cooking Food with
a Quick and Easy Method*

ANNE LOVE

Table of Contents

—
5

Introduction

What is an Instant Pot and how do you use it?

Some people have fallen in love with their Instant Pots. They might love blenders, adore their flaming slow cookers, and need a robot in the kitchen, but the Instant Pot is the one they can't live without anymore.

What is an Instant Pot?

It's a small appliance with huge potential, and in the size of a large pot, it packs an electronic pressure cooker, slow cooker, rice cooker, and yogurt maker. Ingenious isn't it?

If you are already the proud owner of a traditional pressure cooker that is now keeping company with a dust colony in the back of the last kitchen cabinet because of the fear you have that it will explode in your hand, I feel like reassuring you immediately. What makes this new generation of digital pressure cookers different are just the safety features, including sensors that keep track of temperature and pressure level.

All you have to do is connect it to electricity and push a button, the instant pot will do it all by itself. It's as simple to use as the slow cooker, only the cooking times are significantly less.

But what does this thing do that's special?

For one, it cooks whole pieces of meat divinely and super fast. After just under 90 minutes, an entire pork shoulder is so tender that it can be cut with a breadstick, and it tastes amazing, too. The same recipe made with a slow cooker takes about 7 hours to achieve the same result and still the meat isn't as juicy and flavorful. The key to being happy with your electric pressure cooker is to choose recipes where you need to get a smooth and juicy result.

What the Instant Pot looks like

It is a large stainless steel pressure cooker with different capacities (and different prices depending on which one you choose), it has a lid and lots of buttons that will help you set the program you prefer, decide the temperature and the time you want it to start cooking. This is in case you want it to prepare dinner when you are not there and find it ready as soon as you cross the threshold of the house. It is easy to wash because inside the appliance there is a removable stainless steel pot, which you can remove and wash and even use on the stove if you miss one. Inside the package, you will also find a steel basket if you want to try steaming. And the instruction booklet. I know we live in an age where it is no longer used to stop and read how to use something, we are all learned, but do it because this thing is very easy to use but not as intuitive. It only takes 5 minutes for the basic functions. Invest this time for the sake of your future dinners. Don't be fooled by the name, because Instant is just that, the name. It's a quick way to prepare recipes that would otherwise take a lot of time and energy to make. But you must calculate the downtime well. Once the pot is closed it must come under pressure, and it will take at least 15 minutes, when it has finished cooking your food it must slowly release the steam safely before opening, and even for this operation count about ten minutes. However, I feel like I can tell you from the results you get, that the game is worth the candle.

How much what the Instant Pot?

The cost depends a lot on which model you want to buy. The basic model has all the features you need to start cooking with an electric pressure stove, the only thing you can't prepare with the basic model is yogurt which is available from the slightly higher model, the Duo. The Duo Plus is the best-selling model of all since it can also prepare cakes, cook eggs and even sterilize food, and it costs twice as much as the basic model. Then some ultra-technological models have buttons to customize the cooking endlessly, Bluetooth, apps, programming complex recipes, and so on. I'm still of the opinion that to start with, the basic model will bring you joy.

But what do I cook in this Instant Pot?

In this pot of wonders, you can cook all the meat you can think of. Especially large cuts, which would take a long time to cook the traditional way. For example, you could try cooking veal with tuna sauce, even trying the low-temperature function. In addition to the old-fashioned way, you could also try your hand at more daring preparations such as veal ravioli with tuna sauce. You will also obtain fantastic results with braised meats, and I recommend trying braised veal in Barolo wine. But if you're not in the mood for meat, you can always use your digital pressure cooker to cook lentils and turn them into a delicious soup as well. You can prepare whole chicken in it, but be sure to remember to use the sauté function. It will be your special tool for cooking meatloaf. You can also prepare potatoes, especially if they are meant to be mashed.

In this book, you have several very appetizing recipes to use with your Instant Pot. Once you gain skill and experience in using this fantastic appliance, you won't be able to do without it. Enjoy!

Chicken

Turkey and Green Bean Soup

(Ready in about 25 minutes | Servings 4)

Per serving: 295 Calories; 12.2g Fat; 16.4g Carbs; 30.6g Protein; 8.4g
Sugars

Ingredients
1 pound turkey breasts, boneless, skinless and diced
2 cups water
2 cups chicken stock
2 tablespoons apple cider vinegar
1 (28-ounce) can diced tomatoes
1 yellow onion, chopped
2 cloves garlic, minced
2 carrots, diced
1 teaspoon dried oregano
1/2 teaspoon dried marjoram
1/2 teaspoon dried thyme
1/2 teaspoon ground cumin
Salt and ground black pepper, to taste
12 ounces green beans, cut into halves

Directions
Place all of the above ingredients, except for the green beans, into the
Instant Pot.
Secure the lid. Choose the "Poultry" mode and High pressure; cook for
15 minutes. Oncecooking is complete, use a quick pressure release;
carefully remove the lid.
Then, stir in the green beans. Seal the lid again; let it sit for 5 minutes to
blanch the green beans.Bon appétit

Classic Coq au Vin

(Ready in about 25 minutes | Servings 4)

Per serving: 255 Calories; 12.1g Fat; 6.9g Carbs; 29.2g Protein; 2.7g Sugars

Ingredients

1 teaspoons peanut oil

2 chicken drumettes

1 chicken breast

2 shallots, chopped

2 cloves garlic, crushed

1/2 pound chestnut mushrooms, halved

1 cup vegetable stock

1/3 cup red wine

Sea salt and ground black pepper, to your liking

1/2 teaspoon red pepper flakes

1/4 teaspoon curry powder

1/4 cup tomato puree

2 teaspoons all-purpose flour

2 sprigs fresh thyme, leaves picked

Directions

Press the "Sauté" button and heat the peanut oil. Add the chicken, skin-side down, and cook for 7minutes or until browned; reserve. Now, add the shallots and sauté until they're tender and fragrant. Now, stir in the garlic andmushrooms, and cook until aromatic.

Add 1/2 cup of the vegetable stock and red wine, and scrape the bottom of your Instant Pot toloosen any stuck-on bits.

Add the salt, black pepper, red pepper flakes, and curry powder; continue to cook, stirringconstantly.

Now, add the reserved chicken, tomato puree and the remaining 1/2 cup of vegetable stock.Sprinkle with all-purpose flour and fresh thyme leaves. Secure the lid. Choose the "Manual" and cook at High pressure for 11 minutes. Once cooking iscomplete, use a quick pressure release; carefully remove the lid. Bon appétit!

Cheddar and Chicken Bake

(Ready in about 30 minutes | Servings 6)

Per serving: 424 Calories; 28.7g Fat; 7.2g Carbs; 33.2g Protein; 2.8g Sugars

Ingredients

1 tablespoons butter

1 ½ pounds chicken breasts

2 garlic cloves, halved

1 teaspoon cayenne pepper

1/2 teaspoon mustard powder

Sea salt, to taste

1/2 teaspoon ground black pepper

8 ounces Cheddar cheese, sliced

1/2 cup mayonnaise

1 cup Parmesan cheese, grated

Directions

Press the "Sauté" button to heat up the Instant Pot. Melt the butter; sear the chicken for 2 to 3minutes per side.

Add the garlic and continue to sauté for 30 seconds more. Season with cayenne pepper, mustardpowder, salt, and black pepper.

Add the cheddar cheese and mayonnaise; top with grated Parmesan cheese.

Secure the lid. Choose the "Meat/Stew" mode and High pressure; cook for 20 minutes. Oncecooking is complete, use a quick pressure release; carefully remove the lid. Bon appétit!

Chicken Sausage Chowder with Spinach

(Ready in about 15 minutes | Servings 8)

Per serving: 360 Calories; 28.1g Fat; 7.8g Carbs; 19.1g Protein; 2.7g Sugars

Ingredients

1 tablespoon lard, melted

8 ounces chicken sausage, cooked and thinly sliced

1/2 cup scallions, chopped

1 teaspoon ginger garlic paste

1 pound cauliflower, chopped into florets

4 cups vegetable broth

1 pinch red pepper flakes Kosher salt, to taste

1/2 teaspoon freshly ground black pepper, to taste

1 cup spinach, torn into pieces

Directions

Add all ingredients, except for the spinach, to your Instant Pot.

Secure the lid. Choose the "Manual" setting and cook for 9 minutes under High pressure. Oncecooking is complete, use a quick pressure release; carefully remove the lid.

Puree the mixture in your food processor.

Afterwards, add the spinach and seal the lid. Let it stand until the spinach is wilted. Serve inindividual bowls. Enjoy!

Pork

Vermouth Pork Shanks with Vegetables

(Ready in about 40 minutes | Servings 4)

Per serving: 348 Calories; 25.1g Fat; 12.1g Carbs; 17.3g Protein; 4.5g Sugars

Ingredients
1 teaspoons olive oil
1 pound pork shanks, trimmed of skin
1 teaspoon turmeric powder
2 tablespoons vermouth
1 carrot, sliced
1 celery stalk, chopped
1 parsnip, sliced
1 bell pepper, deveined and sliced
1 serrano pepper, deveined and sliced
Sea salt and ground black pepper, to taste
1 teaspoon red pepper flakes, crushed
1 teaspoon garlic powder
1 cup beef bone broth
2 bay leaves

Directions
Press the "Sauté" button to preheat your Instant Pot; heat the olive oil. Once hot, cook the porkshanks until they are delicately browned.
Stir in the remaining ingredients.
Secure the lid. Choose the "Meat/Stew" setting and cook at High pressure for 35 minutes. Oncecooking is complete, use a natural pressure release; carefully remove the lid.
Serve warm over mashed potatoes and enjoy!

Easy Pork Soup with Corn

(Ready in about 15 minutes | Servings 4)

Per serving: 358 Calories; 9.1g Fat; 32.4g Carbs; 36.1g Protein; 0.8g Sugars

Ingredients
1 tablespoon olive oil
1/2 cup onion, chopped
1 pound pork stew meat, cubed
4 cups water
1/4 teaspoon bay leaf, ground
1/2 teaspoon dried basil
1 teaspoon celery seeds
1 cup corn, torn into pieces

Directions
Press the "Sauté" button to preheat your Instant Pot. Heat the olive oil; cook the onion untiltender and translucent.
Add the pork and continue to cook until it is delicately browned. Add the water, ground bay leaf,basil, and celery seeds to the Instant Pot.
Secure the lid. Choose the "Manual" setting and cook at High pressure for 8 minutes. Oncecooking is complete, use a quick pressure release; carefully remove the lid.
Stir in the corn kernels; seal the lid and allow it to sit in the residual heat until the corn is warmedthrough. Serve in individual bowls and enjoy!

Spicy Paprika and Pork Omelet

(Ready in about 25 minutes | Servings 2)

Per serving: 449 Calories; 33.6g Fat; 4.3g Carbs; 32.2g Protein; 1.6g Sugars

Ingredients
1 tablespoon canola oil
1/2 pound ground pork
1 yellow onion, thinly sliced
1 red chili pepper, minced
4 eggs, whisked
1/2 teaspoon garlic powder
1/3 teaspoon cumin powder
1 teaspoon oyster sauce
Kosher salt and ground black pepper, to taste
1/2 teaspoon paprika

Directions
Press the "Sauté" button and heat the oil until sizzling; once hot, cook the ground pork until nolonger pink, crumbling with a spatula.
Add the onion and pepper; cook an additional 2 minutes. Whisk the eggs with the remainingingredients. Pour the egg mixture over the meat mixture in the inner pot.
Secure the lid. Choose the "Manual" mode and cook for 8 minutes at High pressure. Once cooking is complete, use a natural pressure release for 10 minutes; carefully remove the lid. Bonappétit!

Beef

Roast Beef in Sage-Merlot Sauce

(Ready in about 50 minutes | Servings 6)

Per serving: 283 Calories; 12.2g Fat; 5.4g Carbs; 30.9g Protein; 2.1g Sugars

Ingredients

1 teaspoons lard, at room temperature
1 ½ pounds beef roast
1 red onion, chopped
2 garlic cloves, smashed
1 carrot, chopped
1 celery stalk, diced
1 cup water
1/2 cups Merlot Sea salt, to taste
1/2 teaspoon ground black pepper
1 teaspoon paprika
2 bay leaves
1 tablespoon fresh sage
1 tablespoon soy sauce
1 teaspoon butter
1/4 cup fresh chives, chopped

Directions

Press the "Sauté" button to preheat the Instant Pot. Melt the lard and sear the beef until it isbrowned on all sides. Add the onion, garlic, carrot, celery, water, merlot, salt, black pepper, paprika, bay leaves, sage,and soy sauce. Secure the lid. Choose the "Meat/Stew" mode and High pressure; cook for 40 minutes. Once cooking is complete, use a natural pressure release; carefully remove the lid.Transfer the roast to a cutting board; allow it to cool slightly before slicing. Press the "Sauté" button and let it simmer until the sauce is reduced. Stir in the butter and press the "Cancel" button. Spoon the sauce over the sliced beef. Serve garnished with fresh chives and enjoy

---

Spicy Beef in White Rum Sauce

(Ready in about 25 minutes | Servings 6)

Per serving: 293 Calories; 15.6g Fat; 4.3g Carbs; 27.3g Protein; 0.9g Sugars

Ingredients

1 tablespoons olive oil

1 ½ pounds beef flank steak

Sea salt and freshly ground black pepper, to taste

1 teaspoon cayenne pepper

1 teaspoon dried marjoram

1/2 teaspoon dried thyme

1/2 teaspoon dried basil

1/4 cup white rum

1 cup water

2 bell peppers, deveined and chopped

1 Chile de Arbol, deveined and minced

1 shallot, halved and sliced

1 cup sour cream

Directions

Press the "Sauté" button to preheat your Instant Pot. Then, heat the oil until sizzling. Once hot, cook the beef until browned on all sides.

Add the seasonings. Deglaze the inner pot with white rum and add the water, peppers, and shallot.

Secure the lid. Choose the "Poultry" setting and cook at High pressure for 15 minutes. Once cooking is complete, use a quick pressure release; carefully remove the lid.

Transfer the meat to a cutting board; slice the beef against the grain.

Now, fold in the sour cream and press the "Sauté" button; let it simmer until the cooking liquid is thoroughly warmed and reduced. Serve warm.

Cheesy Meatballs in Mushroom Sauce

(Ready in about 10 minutes | Servings 6)

Per serving: 450 Calories; 24g Fat; 26.7g Carbs; 27.8g Protein; 9.9g Sugars

Ingredients
1 pound ground beef
2 slices bacon, chopped
1/2 cup Romano cheese, grated
1 cup seasoned breadcrumbs
1/2 cup scallions, chopped
2 garlic cloves, crushed
2 large eggs, beaten
1/3 cup milk
1 tablespoon canola oil
1 (10 ¼-ounce) can condensed mushroom soup
1 cup tomato paste

Directions
Thoroughly combine the ground beef, bacon, cheese, breadcrumbs, scallions, garlic, eggs, andmilk. Roll the mixture into meatballs.
Press the "Sauté" button to preheat the Instant Pot. Heat the oil and sear the meatballs until theyare browned on all sides.
Add the canned mushroom soup and tomato paste to the Instant Pot. Secure the lid. Choose the "Manual" mode and High pressure; cook for 6 minutes. Once cookingis complete, use a quick pressure release; carefully remove the lid.
Serve warm, garnished with mashed potatoes. Bon appétit!

Classic Ground Beef Tacos

(Ready in about 30 minutes | Servings 4)

Per serving: 618 Calories; 37.8g Fat; 21g Carbs; 47.1g Protein; 4.4g Sugars

Ingredients
1 tablespoon canola oil
1 ½ pounds ground beef
1 onion, chopped
2 peppers, deseeded and sliced
1 chili pepper, minced
4 garlic cloves, minced1 teaspoon marjoram
1 teaspoon Mexican oregano
Kosher salt and ground black pepper, to taste
1 teaspoon cumin powder
1/2 teaspoon red pepper flakes
1 teaspoon mustard seeds
12 small taco shells
1 head lettuce
1/2 cup chunky salsa
1/2 cup sour cream

Direction
Press the "Sauté" button to preheat your Instant Pot. Heat the oil and sear the ground chuck for 2to 3 minutes or until mostly brown.
Add the onion, peppers, garlic, and spices to the inner pot.
Secure the lid. Choose the "Manual" mode and cook for 10 minutes at High pressure. Oncecooking is complete, use a natural pressure release; carefully remove the lid.
Press the "Sauté" button and cook, stirring continuously, until the liquid has almost evaporatedor about 10 minutes.
To assemble your tacos, layer the beef mixture and lettuce in each taco shell. Serve with the salsaand sour cream. Enjoy!

Soups

Chicken Tortilla Soup

(Ready in about 25 minutes | Servings 4)

Per serving: 428 Calories; 27.2g Fat; 30.7g Carbs; 19.8g Protein; 6.4g Sugars

Ingredients

2 tablespoons olive oil

1/2 cup shallots, chopped

1 sweet pepper, chopped

1 Poblano chili pepper, chopped

1/2 pound chicken thighs, boneless and skinless

2 ripe tomatoes, chopped

1 can (10-ounce) red enchilada sauce

2 teaspoons ground cumin

1 teaspoon ground coriander

1 teaspoon chili powder

Seasoned salt and freshly cracked pepper, to taste

4 cups roasted vegetable broth

1 bay leaf

1 can (15-ounce) black beans, drained and rinsed

4 (6-inch) corn tortillas, cut crosswise into 1/4-inch strips

1 avocado, cut into 1/2-inch dice

1 cup cheddar cheese, shredded

Directions

Press the "Sauté" button and heat the olive oil. Once hot, sauté the shallots and peppers untiltender and aromatic.

Add the chicken thighs, tomatoes, enchilada sauce, cumin, coriander, chili powder, salt, blackpepper, vegetable broth, and bay leaf to the inner pot.

Secure the lid. Choose the "Manual" mode and cook for 8 minutes at High pressure. Once cooking is complete, use a natural pressure release for 10 minutes; carefully remove the lid.

Stir in the canned beans and seal the lid; let it sit in the residual heat until everything is heatedthrough.

Divide your soup between individual bowls and serve garnished with tortilla strips, avocado, andcheddar cheese.

Old-Fashioned Ham Bone Soup

(Ready in about 30 minutes | Servings 5)

Per serving: 197 Calories; 10.2g Fat; 9.3g Carbs; 17.7g Protein; 3.7g Sugars

Ingredients
2 tablespoons olive oil

1/2 cup onion, chopped

2 carrots, diced

1 rib celery, diced

1 parsnip, diced

1 ham bone

5 cups chicken stock

Sea salt and ground black pepper, to taste

Directions
Press the "Sauté" button and heat the olive oil until sizzling. Then, sauté the onion, carrot, celery,and parsnip until tender.

Add the ham bone, chicken stock, salt, and black pepper to the inner pot.

Secure the lid. Choose the "Manual" mode and cook for 15 minutes at High pressure. Oncecooking is complete, use a natural pressure release for 10 minutes; carefully remove the lid.

Remove the ham bone from the inner pot. Chop the meat from the bone; add back into the soup.Serve in individual bowls and enjoy!

Simple Clam Chowder

(Ready in about 15 minutes | Servings 4)

Per serving: 349 Calories; 18.4g Fat; 41.1g Carbs; 7.3g Protein; 8.4g Sugars

Ingredients
1 tablespoons butter
1 onion, chopped
1 garlic clove, minced
1 stalk celery, diced
1 carrot, diced
1cup water
2 cups fish stock
Sea salt and white pepper, to taste
1 pound Russet potatoes, peeled and diced
1 teaspoon cayenne pepper
18 ounces canned clams, chopped with juice
1 cup heavy cream

Directions
Press the "Sauté" button and melt the butter; once hot, cook the onion, garlic, celery, and carrotfor 3 minutes or until they have softened.
Add the water, stock, salt, white pepper, potatoes, and cayenne pepper. Secure the lid. Choose the "Manual" mode and cook for 2 minutes at High pressure. Oncecooking is complete, use a quick pressure release; carefully remove the lid.
Press the "Sauté" button and use the lowest setting. Stir in the clams and heavy cream. Let itsimmer for about 5 minutes or until everything is thoroughly heated. Bon appétit!

Mediterranean-Style Lima Bean Soup

(Ready in about 25 minutes | Servings 5)

Per serving: 263 Calories; 8.1g Fat; 35.7g Carbs; 15.4g Protein; 10.1g Sugars

Ingredients

2 tablespoons sesame oil
1 pound cremini mushrooms, thinly sliced
1 large-sized eggplant, sliced into rounds
1 red onion, chopped
2 garlic cloves, chopped
2 carrots, sliced
2 sweet potatoes, peeled and diced
1/2 teaspoon red curry paste
1/2 teaspoon cayenne pepper
Sea salt and ground black pepper, to taste
2 sprigs thyme
2 sprigs rosemary
2 medium-sized tomatoes, pureed
5 cups roasted vegetable broth
16 ounces lima beans, soaked overnight
Juice of 1 fresh lemon

Directions

Press the "Sauté" button and heat the oil until sizzling. Now, cook the mushrooms, eggplant,onion, and garlic until just tender and fragrant. Add the carrots, sweet potatoes, curry paste, spices, tomatoes, broth, and lima beans.

Secure the lid. Choose the "Manual" mode and cook for 13 minutes at High pressure. Oncecooking is complete, use a quick pressure release; carefully remove the lid.

Divide your soup between individual bowls; add a few drizzles of lemon juice to each servingand enjoy!

Stews

Beef Stew with Green Peas

(Ready in about 35 minutes | Servings 4)

Per serving: 540 Calories; 29g Fat; 25.5g Carbs; 44.7g Protein; 10.7g Sugars

Ingredients

1 tablespoons olive oil
1 ½ pounds beef stew meat, cut bite-sized pieces
1 red onion, chopped
4 cloves garlic, minced
1 carrot, cut into rounds
1 parsnip, cut into rounds
2 stalks celery, diced
Sea salt and ground black pepper, to taste
1 teaspoon cayenne pepper
4 cups beef bone broth
1/2 cup tomato paste
1 tablespoon fish sauce
2 bay leaves
1 cup frozen green peas

Directions

Press the "Sauté" button and heat the oil. Once hot, brown the beef stew meat for 4 to 5 minutes;set aside. Then, cook the onion in pan drippings until tender and translucent; stir in the garlic and cook an additional 30 seconds or until aromatic. Add the carrots, parsnip, celery, salt, black pepper, cayenne pepper, beef broth, tomato paste, fishsauce, and bay leaves. Stir in the reserved beef stew meat. Secure the lid. Choose the "Meat/Stew" mode and cook for 20 minutes at High pressure. Oncecooking is complete, use a quick pressure release; carefully remove the lid. Stir in the green peas, cover, and let it sit in the residual heat until warmed through or 5 to 7minutes. Serve and enjoy!

Smoked Sausage and Bean Stew

(Ready in about 40 minutes | Servings 4)

Per serving: 396 Calories; 21.8g Fat; 25.8g Carbs; 6.2g Protein; 14.7g Sugars

Ingredients
1 tablespoon olive oil
10 ounces smoked beef sausage, sliced
2 carrots, chopped
1 onion, chopped
2 garlic cloves, minced
Sea salt and ground black pepper, to taste
1/2 teaspoon fresh rosemary, chopped
1 teaspoon fresh basil, chopped
1 cup canned tomatoes, crushed
1 cup chicken broth
20 ounces pinto beans, soaked overnight
6 ounces kale, torn into pieces

Directions
Press the "Sauté" button and heat the oil. Once hot, brown the sausage for 3 to 4 minutes.Add the remaining ingredients, except for the kale, to the inner pot.
Secure the lid. Choose the "Bean/Chili" mode and cook for 25 minutes at High pressure. Oncecooking is complete, use a quick pressure release; carefully remove the lid.
Next, stir in the kale and seal the lid. Let it sit for 5 minutes before serving. Bon appétit!

Vegan Pottage Stew

(Ready in about 15 minutes | Servings 4)

Per serving: 315 Calories; 11.1g Fat; 41.6g Carbs; 12.8g Protein; 5.7g Sugars

Ingredients
2 tablespoons olive oil
1 onion, chopped
2 garlic cloves, minced
2 carrots, diced
2 parsnips, diced
1 turnip, diced
4 cups vegetable broth
2 bay leaves
2 thyme sprigs
2 rosemary sprigs
Kosher salt and freshly ground black pepper, to taste
1/4 cup red wine
1 cup porridge oats

Directions
Press the "Sauté" button and heat the olive oil until sizzling. Now, sauté the onion and garlicuntil just tender and fragrant.
Add the remaining ingredients to the inner pot; stir to combine.
Secure the lid. Choose the "Manual" mode and cook for 10 minutes at High pressure. Oncecooking is complete, use a quick pressure release; carefully remove the lid.
Ladle into individual bowls and serve immediately. Bon appétit

Mediterranean Chicken Stew

(Ready in about 35 minutes | Servings 4)

Per serving: 400 Calories; 27.9g Fat; 11.3g Carbs; 24.6g Protein; 5.1g Sugars

Ingredients

2 tablespoons olive oil

1 onion, chopped

1 stalk celery, chopped

2 carrots, chopped

1 teaspoon garlic, minced

4 chicken legs, boneless skinless

1/4 cup dry red wine

2 ripe tomatoes, pureed

2 cups chicken bone broth

2 bay leaves

Sea salt and ground black pepper, to taste

1/2 teaspoon dried basil

1 teaspoon dried oregano

1/2 cup Kalamata olives, pitted and sliced

Directions

Press the "Sauté" button and heat the oil. Now, sauté the onion, celery, and carrot for 4 to 5minutes or until they are tender.

Add the other ingredients, except for the Kalamata olives, and stir to combine.

Secure the lid. Choose the "Manual" mode. Cook for 15 minutes at High pressure. Once cookingis complete, use a natural pressure release for 10 minutes; carefully remove the lid.

Serve warm garnished with Kalamata olives. Bon appétit!

Stocks & Sauces

Homemade Shrimp Stock

(Ready in about 55 minutes | Servings 8)

Per serving: 69 Calories; 6.7g Fat; 1.9g Carbs; 0.3g Protein; 0.7g Sugars

Ingredients
Shrimp shells from 3 pounds shrimp
8 cups water
1/2 cup cilantro, chopped
2 celery stalks, diced
4 cloves garlic
1 onion, quartered
1 teaspoon mixed peppercorns
1 tablespoon sea salt
2 bay leaves
4 tablespoons olive oil

Directions
Add all ingredients to the inner pot.
Secure the lid. Choose the "Soup/Broth" mode and cook for 30 minutes at High pressure. Oncecooking is complete, use a natural pressure release for 10 minutes; carefully remove the lid.
Strain the shrimp shells and vegetables using a colander. Bon appétit!

Chicken and Vegetable Stock

(Ready in about 1 hour 10 minutes | Servings 9)

Per serving: 79 Calories; 2.9g Fat; 2.6g Carbs; 21.9g Protein; 1.2g Sugars

Ingredients
1 chicken carcass
2 carrots, cut into 2-inch pieces
1 celery rib, cut into 2-inch pieces
1 large onion, quartered
Sea salt, to taste
1 teaspoon mixed peppercorns
1 bay leaf
1 bunch parsley
9 cups cold water

Directions
Place all ingredients in the inner pot.
Secure the lid. Choose the "Soup/Broth" mode and cook for 40 minutes at High pressure. Oncecooking is complete, use a natural pressure release for 20 minutes; carefully remove the lid.
Remove the bones and vegetables with a slotted spoon. Use immediately or store for later use.Bon appétit!

20-Minute Chicken Ragù

(Ready in about 20 minutes | Servings 4)

Per serving: 431 Calories; 18g Fat; 33.7g Carbs; 29.1g Protein; 17.1g Sugars

Ingredients
2 tablespoons olive oil
1 pound ground chicken
1 onion, chopped
2 cloves garlic, minced
1/4 cup dry red wine
1 stalk celery, chopped
1 bell pepper, chopped
1 teaspoon fresh basil, chopped
1 teaspoon fresh rosemary, chopped
1 teaspoon cayenne pepper
Salt and fresh ground pepper to taste
2 cups tomato sauce
1 cup chicken bone broth

Directions
Press the "Sauté" button and heat the oil. When the oil starts to sizzle, cook the ground chickenuntil no longer pink; crumble it with a wooden spatula.
Add the onion and garlic to the browned chicken; let it cook for a minute or so. Add a splash ofwine to deglaze the pan.
Stir in the remaining ingredients.
Secure the lid. Choose the "Manual" mode and cook for 6 minutes at High pressure. Once cooking is complete, use a natural pressure release for 10 minutes; carefully remove the lid. Bonappétit!

Eggplant Light Sauce with Wine

(Ready in about 10 minutes | Servings 6)

Per serving: 147 Calories; 10.4g Fat; 9.3g Carbs; 5.2g Protein; 4.6g Sugars

Ingredients
1 tablespoons olive oil
1 pound eggplants, sliced
4 garlic cloves, minced
2 tomatoes, chopped
1 cup white wine
1 teaspoon oregano
1/2 teaspoon rosemary
1 teaspoon basil
Sea salt and ground black pepper, to taste
2 tablespoons tahini (sesame butter)
1/2 cup Romano cheese, freshly grated

Directions
Press the "Sauté" button and heat the olive oil. Then, cook the eggplant slices until they arecharred at the bottom. Work with batches.
Add the garlic, tomatoes, wine, and spices.
Secure the lid. Choose the "Bean/Chili" mode and cook for 3 minutes at High pressure. Oncecooking is complete, use a quick pressure release; carefully remove the lid.
Press the "Sauté" button again to thicken the cooking liquid. Add the tahini paste and stir tocombine. Top with Romano cheese and serve.

Fish & Seafood

Curried Halibut Steaks

(Ready in about 15 minutes | Servings 4)

Per serving: 325 Calories; 10.7g Fat; 17.2g Carbs; 38.6g Protein; 6.5g Sugars

Ingredients

1 tablespoon olive oil
1 cup scallions, chopped
1/2 cup beef bone broth
1 pound halibut steaks, rinsed and cubed
1 cup tomato purée
1 jalapeño pepper, seeded and minced
1 teaspoon ginger garlic paste
1 tablespoon red curry paste
1/2 teaspoon ground cumin
1 cup coconut milk, unsweetened
Salt and ground black pepper, to taste

Directions

Press the "Sauté" button to preheat your Instant Pot. Now, heat the olive oil; cook the scallionsuntil tender and fragrant.
Then, use the broth to deglaze the bottom of the inner pot. Stir in the remaining ingredients.
Secure the lid. Choose the "Manual" mode and Low pressure; cook for 7 minutes. Once cookingis complete, use a quick pressure release; carefully remove the lid.
Taste, adjust the seasonings and serve right now.

Baked Fish with Parmesan

(Ready in about 15 minutes | Servings 4)

Per serving: 376 Calories; 22.1g Fat; 9.4g Carbs; 34.2g Protein; 0.8g Sugars

Ingredients
2 ripe tomatoes, sliced
1 teaspoon dried rosemary
1 teaspoon dried marjoram
1/2 teaspoon dried thyme
4 mahi-mahi fillets
2 tablespoons butter, at room temperature
Sea salt and ground black pepper, to taste
8 ounces Parmesan cheese, freshly grated

Directions
Add 1 ½ cups of water and a rack to your Instant Pot.
Spritz a casserole dish with a nonstick cooking spray. Arrange the slices of tomatoes on thebottom of the dish. Add the herbs.
Place the mahi-mahi fillets on the top; drizzle the melted butter over the fish. Season it with saltand black pepper. Place the baking dish on the rack.
Secure the lid. Choose the "Manual" mode and Low pressure; cook for 9 minutes. Once cookingis complete, use a quick pressure release; carefully remove the lid.
Top with parmesan and seal the lid again; allow the cheese to melt and serve.

Chunky Tilapia Stew

(Ready in about 15 minutes | Servings 4)

Per serving: 221 Calories; 9.3g Fat; 4.9g Carbs; 25g Protein; 1.8g Sugars

Ingredients

2 tablespoons sesame oil

1 cup scallions, chopped

2 garlic cloves, minced

1/3 cup dry vermouth

1 cup shellfish stock

2 cups water

2 ripe plum tomatoes, crushed

Sea salt, to taste

1/4 teaspoon freshly ground black pepper, or more to taste

1 teaspoon hot paprika

1 pound tilapia fillets, boneless, skinless and diced

1 tablespoon fresh lime juice

1 teaspoon dried rosemary

1/2 teaspoon dried oregano

1/2 teaspoon dried basil

Directions

Press the "Sauté" button to preheat your Instant Pot. Heat the oil and sauté the scallions andgarlic until fragrant.

Add a splash of vermouth to deglaze the bottom of the inner pot.

Secure the lid. Choose the "Manual" mode and High pressure; cook for 5 minutes. Once cookingis complete, use a quick pressure release; carefully remove the lid.

Serve with some extra lime slices if desired. Bon appétit!

Easy Lobster Tails with Butter

(Ready in about 10 minutes | Servings 4)

Per serving: 292 Calories; 14.1g Fat; 4.2g Carbs; 35.1g Protein; 0.1g Sugars

Ingredients

1 ½ pounds lobster tails, halved

1/2 stick butter, at room temperature

Sea salt and freshly ground black pepper, to taste

1/2 teaspoon red pepper flakes

Directions

Add a metal trivet, steamer basket, and 1 cup of water in your Instant Pot.Place the lobster tails, shell side down, in the prepared steamer basket.

Secure the lid. Choose the "Steam" mode and cook for 3 minutes at Low pressure. Once cookingis complete, use a quick pressure release; carefully remove the lid.

Drizzle with butter. Season with salt, black pepper, and red pepper and serve immediately.Enjoy!

Beans – Pasta - Grains

The Best Barley Salad Ever

(Ready in about 15 minutes | Servings 4)

Per serving: 582 Calories; 22.1g Fat; 81g Carbs; 17.6g Protein; 6.4g Sugars

Ingredients
1 ½ cups pearl barley
3 cups water
Sea salt and ground black pepper, to taste
1 leek, thinly sliced
2 cloves garlic, crushed
4 tablespoons extra-virgin olive oil
1/2 cup fresh parsley, chopped
2 tablespoons lime juice, freshly squeezed
1/2 cup canned chickpea, rinsed
1 cup pickles, diced
4 ounces feta cheese, crumbled

Directions
Add the barley and water to the Instant Pot.
Secure the lid. Choose the "Manual" mode and High pressure; cook for 9 minutes. Once cookingis complete, use a natural pressure release; carefully remove the lid.
Allow the barley to cool completely; then, transfer it to a salad bowl.
Add the remaining ingredients and toss to combine well. Place in your refrigerator until ready to serve. Enjoy!

Corn on the Cob with Smoky Lime Butter

(Ready in about 15 minutes | Servings 3)

Per serving: 263 Calories; 16.2g Fat; 30.9g Carbs; 4.3g Protein; 1.1g Sugars

Ingredients
1 ¼ cups water
3 ears corn on the cob
1/2 stick butter, softened
A few drops of liquid smoke
1/2 lemon, juiced
1 tablespoon fresh cilantro, minced
A pinch of sugar
Sea salt and white pepper, to taste

Directions
Pour water into the base of your Instant Pot. Place three ears corn on the cob on a metal trivet.Secure the lid.

Choose the "Steam" mode and cook for 3 minutes under High pressure. Once cooking iscomplete, use a natural release; remove the lid carefully. Reserve the corn on the cob.

Press the "Sauté" button to heat up your Instant Pot. Melt the butter and remove from heat. Addthe liquid smoke, lemon juice, cilantro, sugar, sea salt, and pepper; stir to combine.

Toss the corn on the cob with the smoky lemon butter. Bon appétit!

Easy Pearl Barley with Peppers

(Ready in about 30 minutes | Servings 3)

Per serving: 339 Calories; 8.8g Fat; 60.3g Carbs; 7.6g Protein; 5.2g Sugars

Ingredients

1 tablespoon sesame oil

1 yellow onion, chopped

2 garlic cloves, minced

2 bell peppers, seeded and chopped

1 jalapeno pepper, seeded and chopped

1 cups pearl barley, rinsed

2 ½ cups roasted vegetable broth

1/4 cup chives, chopped

Directions

Press the "Sauté" button and heat the oil. Once hot, cook the onion until just tender and fragrantor about 3 minutes.

Stir in the garlic and peppers; continue cooking for 2 minutes more or until they are aromatic.Add the barley and vegetable broth to the inner pot.

Secure the lid. Choose the "Multigrain" mode and cook for 20 minutes at High pressure. Oncecooking is complete, use a quick pressure release; carefully remove the lid.

Fluff the barley with a fork; garnish with chopped chives and serve with your favorite main dish.Bon appétit!

Sorakkai Sambar (Indian Lentil Stew)

(Ready in about 35 minutes | Servings 3)

Per serving: 248 Calories; 7.9g Fat; 36.8g Carbs; 6.9g Protein; 13.4g Sugars

Ingredients
1 cup Pigeon pea lentils
2 teaspoons sesame oil
1 yellow onion, chopped
6 curry leaves
1 Indian ghost jolokia chili pepper, chopped
1 tablespoon tamarind
1 teaspoon Urad Dal
1 tablespoon sambar powder
1 teaspoon turmeric powder
Sea salt and ground black pepper, to taste
1 teaspoon cayenne pepper
1 cup tomato sauce

Directions
Add the lentils and 4 cups of water to the inner pot.
Secure the lid. Choose the "Manual" mode and cook for 10 minutes at High pressure. Oncecooking is complete, use a natural pressure release for 10 minutes; carefully remove the lid.
Meanwhile, heat a saucepan over medium-high heat. Cook the onion for about 3 minutes or untiltranslucent. Now, add the curry leaves and chili pepper to the skillet. Let it cook for a further minute or until they are aromatic.
Add the other ingredients, cover, and reduce the heat to medium-low; let it simmer for about 13minutes or until everything is thoroughly cooked.
Transfer the onion/tomato mixture to the inner pot of your Instant Pot. Stir to combine and serveimmediately. Bon appétit!

—

Low-Carb

Breakfast Casserole with Zucchini and Bacon

(Ready in about 25 minutes | Servings 8)

Per serving: 320 Calories; 24.3g Fat; 5.3g Carbs; 19.7g Protein; 2.9g Sugars

Ingredients
1/2 pound zucchini, grated and squeezed dry
1 white onion, chopped
1 clove garlic, minced
6 slices bacon, chopped
1 cup Colby cheese, shredded
1 cup Cottage cheese, room temperature
8 eggs, beaten
1/2 cup Greek yogurt, room temperature
Sea salt and ground black pepper, to taste
1/4 teaspoon dried marjoram
1/4 teaspoon dried rosemary
1 teaspoon dried parsley flakes

Directions
Start by adding 1 cup of water and a metal trivet to the bottom of your Instant Pot.
Mix the ingredients until everything is well incorporated. Spoon the mixture into a lightlygreased casserole dish.
Lower the casserole dish onto the trivet.
Secure the lid. Choose "Manual" mode and High pressure; cook for 20 minutes. Once cooking iscomplete, use a quick pressure release; carefully remove the lid. Bon appétit!

Mushroom and Cream Cheese Pâté

(Ready in about 10 minutes | Servings 8)

Per serving: 162 Calories; 14.4g Fat; 3.6g Carbs; 3.9g Protein; 2.4g Sugars

Ingredients

3 tablespoons olive oi1 1
pound brown mushrooms, chopped
1/2 yellow onion, chopped
2 garlic cloves, minced
2 tablespoons cognac
Sea salt, to taste
1/3 teaspoon black pepper
1/2 teaspoon cayenne pepper
1 cup cream cheese, at room temperature

Directions

Press the "Sauté" button to heat up the Instant Pot. Now, heat the oil and cook the mushroomswith the onions until softened and fragrant. Stir in the garlic, cognac, salt, black pepper, and cayenne pepper.
Secure the lid. Choose "Manual" mode and High pressure; cook for 5 minutes. Once cooking iscomplete, use a quick pressure release; carefully remove the lid.
Transfer the mixture to a food processor. Add the cream cheese and continue to mix untileverything is well incorporated. Serve with veggie sticks. Bon appétit!

Pork and Green Bean Casserole

(Ready in about 30 minutes | Servings 6)

Per serving: 348 Calories; 23.1g Fat; 8.6g Carbs; 26.3g Protein; 4.4g Sugars

Ingredients

1 pound ground pork
1 yellow onion, thinly sliced
2 garlic cloves, smashed
1 green bell pepper, thinly sliced
1 red bell pepper, thinly sliced
1 habanero chili pepper, thinly sliced
1 cup green beans
3 ripe tomatoes, chopped
1/2 teaspoon cumin, ground
Salt and ground black pepper, to taste
1/2 teaspoon cayenne pepper
1 cup Colby cheese, shredded
2 tablespoons fresh chives, chopped

Directions

Start by adding 1 ½ cups of water and a metal rack to the bottom of your Instant Pot.

Mix the pork, onion, garlic, pepper, green beans, tomatoes, cumin, salt, black pepper, andcayenne pepper until well combined.

Pour the mixture into a lightly greased casserole dish that will fit in your Instant Pot. Then, lowerthe dish onto the rack.

Secure the lid. Choose "Manual" mode and Low pressure; cook for 20 minutes. Once cooking iscomplete, use a quick pressure release; carefully remove the lid.

Top with the Colby cheese and cover with the lid. Let it sit in a residual heat an additional 7 to10 minutes.

Serve garnished with fresh chives. Bon appétit

Mexican-Style Stuffed Peppers

(Ready in about 25 minutes | Servings 4)

Per serving: 407 Calories; 27g Fat; 6.3g Carbs; 32.4g Protein; 3.7g Sugars

Ingredients
1/2 pound ground beef
1/4 pound ground pork
4 eggs, whisked
2 garlic cloves, minced
1/2 cup onion, chopped
Salt and ground black pepper, to taste
1 (1-ounce) package taco seasoning mix
1 cup Cotija cheese, grated
4 bell peppers, remove seeds and cut the tops off
8 ounces canned tomato sauce

Directions
Start by adding 1 cup of water and a metal rack to the bottom of the Instant Pot. Spritz acasserole dish with a nonstick cooking spray.
In a mixing bowl, thoroughly combine the ground meat, eggs, garlic, onion, salt, pepper, tacoseasoning mix, and Cotija cheese.
Fill the peppers with the cheese/meat mixture. Place the peppers on the rack in the Instant Pot.Pour the tomato sauce over the peppers.
Secure the lid. Choose "Manual" mode and High pressure; cook for 20 minutes. Once cooking iscomplete, use a natural pressure release; carefully remove the lid. Bon appétit!

Vegan

Green Pea Medley

(Ready in about 25 minutes | Servings 6)

Per serving: 173 Calories; 6.6g Fat; 22.7g Carbs; 7.7g Protein; 7.9g Sugars

Ingredients

1 tablespoons canola oil

1 teaspoon cumin seeds

2 ½ cups green peas, whole

2 ripe Roma tomatoes, seeded and crushed

3 cups roasted vegetable stock

1 shallot, diced

2 cloves garlic, minced

2 carrots, chopped

2 parsnips, chopped

1 red bell pepper, seeded and chopped

2 bay leaves

Sea salt and ground black pepper, to taste

1 teaspoon cayenne pepper

1/2 teaspoon dried dill

Directions

Press the "Sauté" button to preheat the Instant Pot. Once hot, add the oil. Then, sauté the cuminseeds for 30 seconds.

Add the shallot, garlic, carrots, parsnip and pepper; continue to sauté for 3 to 4 minutes more oruntil vegetables are tender.

Now, stir in the remaining ingredients.

Secure the lid. Choose the "Manual" mode and cook for 18 minutes under High pressure. Oncecooking is complete, use a natural release; carefully remove the lid.

Serve with cream cheese if desired. Bon appétit!

Easy Vegan Risotto

(Ready in about 15 minutes | Servings 2)

Per serving: 291 Calories; 20g Fat; 35.4g Carbs; 11.3g Protein; 2.8g
Sugars

Ingredients

1 tablespoon olive oil
2 garlic cloves, minced
1 white onion, finely chopped
1 cup Arborio rice
1 cup water
1 cup vegetable stock
1/2 teaspoon dried basil
1/2 teaspoon dried oregano
Sea salt and ground black pepper, to taste
1 teaspoon smoked paprika

Directions

Press the "Sauté" button to preheat your Instant Pot. Heat the oil and
sauté the garlic and onionuntil tender and fragrant or about 3 minutes.
Add the remaining ingredients; stir to combine well.
Secure the lid. Choose the "Manual" mode and cook for 5 minutes
under High pressure. Oncecooking is complete, use a quick release;
carefully remove the lid.
Ladle into individual bowls and serve warm. Enjoy!

Vegan Lentil and Tomato Bowl

(Ready in about 20 minutes | Servings 4)

Per serving: 405 Calories; 5.9g Fat; 67.5g Carbs; 24.5g Protein; 3.8g Sugars

Ingredients
1 tablespoon olive oil
2 cups red lentils
1/2 cup scallions, finely chopped
1 teaspoon garlic, minced
1 teaspoon turmeric powder
Sea salt and ground black pepper, to taste
1 teaspoon sweet paprika
1 (15-ounce) can tomatoes, crushed
1 bay leaf
1 handful fresh cilantro leaves, chopped

Directions
Add the olive oil, lentils, scallions, garlic, turmeric, salt, black pepper, paprika, tomatoes, andbay leaf to your Instant Pot.
Secure the lid. Choose the "Manual" mode and cook for 12 minutes under High pressure. Oncecooking is complete, use a natural release; carefully remove the lid.
Discard the bay leaf and spoon the lentil into serving bowls. Serve topped with fresh cilantro.Enjoy!

Summer Zucchini Bowl

(Ready in about 15 minutes | Servings 4)

Per serving: 143 Calories; 9.4g Fat; 12.7g Carbs; 5.6g Protein; 4.4g Sugars

Ingredients
1 tablespoons garlic-infused olive oil
1 garlic clove, minced
1/2 cup scallions, chopped1 pound zucchini, sliced
1/2 cup tomato paste
1/2 cup vegetable broth
Salt, to taste
1/2 teaspoon ground black pepper
1/2 teaspoon dried oregano
1/2 teaspoon dried basil
1 teaspoon paprika
1/2 cup Kalamata olives, pitted and sliced

Directions
Press the "Sauté" button to preheat the Instant Pot. Now, heat the oil; sauté the garlic andscallions for 2 minutes or until they are tender and fragrant.

Add the zucchini, tomato paste, broth, salt, black pepper, oregano, basil, and paprika.

Secure the lid. Choose the "Manual" mode and Low pressure; cook for 4 minutes. Once cookingis complete, use a quick pressure release; carefully remove the lid.

Serve garnished with Kalamata olives. Bon appétit!

Vegetable & Side Dishes

Mashed Potatoes with Spring Garlic and Sour Cream

(Ready in about 15 minutes | Servings 4)

Per serving: 230 Calories; 14g Fat; 23.3g Carbs; 3.8g Protein; 1.7g Sugars

Ingredients
1 cup water
1 pound Yukon Gold potatoes, peeled and cubed
1/2 stick butter, softened
2 tablespoons spring garlic, minced
1/4 cup milk
1/3 cup sour cream
1/2 teaspoon dried oregano
1/2 teaspoon dried rosemary
1/2 teaspoon paprika
Salt and ground black pepper, to taste

Directions
Add 1 cup of water and steamer basket to the base of your Instant Pot. Place the cubed potatoes in the steamer basket; transfer it to the Instant Pot. Secure the lid. Selectthe "Manual" mode; cook for 4 minutes under High pressure.

Once cooking is complete, use a quick release; carefully remove the lid. Meanwhile, heat a pan over a moderate heat. Melt the butter and cook the spring garlic until it istender and aromatic.

Add the milk and scrape up any browned bits with a spatula. Allow it to cool slightly.

In a mixing bowl, mash the cooked potatoes. Add the butter/garlic mixture along with the otheringredients.

Taste, adjust the seasonings and serve warm. Bon appétit!

Potatoes Au Gratin

(Ready in about 20 minutes | Servings 4)

Per serving: 440 Calories; 16.2g Fat; 58g Carbs; 16.5g Protein; 3.9g Sugars

Ingredients

6 medium potatoes, peeled and thinly sliced
1 cup vegetable broth
1 shallot, chopped
2 garlic cloves, sliced
1/2 teaspoon dried basil
Sea salt and ground black pepper, to taste
1/2 teaspoon paprika
1/2 cup heavy cream
1 cup Romano cheese, preferably freshly grated

Directions

Arrange the sliced potatoes on the bottom of a lightly greased inner pot. Add the vegetable broth,shallot, garlic, basil, salt, black pepper and paprika to the inner pot.
Secure the lid. Choose the "Manual" mode and cook for 4 minutes at High pressure. Oncecooking is complete, use a quick pressure release; carefully remove the lid.
Preheat your oven to broil. Transfer the potatoes to an oven-safe dish. Top with the heavy creamand Romano cheese.
Broil until the cheese is bubbling and golden brown. Let it sit on a cooling rack for 5 minutesbefore slicing and serving. Enjoy!

Garlicky Green Beans

(Ready in about 10 minutes | Servings 4)

Per serving: 117 Calories; 7.2g Fat; 12.6g Carbs; 3.3g Protein; 5.6g Sugars

Ingredients
2 tablespoons olive oil
2 garlic cloves, minced
1 ½ pounds green beans, trimmed
Salt and freshly ground black pepper, to taste
1 teaspoon cayenne pepper
2 tablespoons fresh chives, chopped

Directions
Press the "Sauté" button and heat the oil until sizzling. Now, sauté the garlic until tender but notbrowned.
Add the green beans, salt, black pepper, and cayenne pepper to the inner pot. Pour in 1 cup ofwater.
Secure the lid. Choose the "Manual" mode and cook for 3 minutes at High pressure. Oncecooking is complete, use a quick pressure release; carefully remove the lid.
Garnish with fresh chives and serve warm.

Easy and Healthy Vegetable Mash

(Ready in about 10 minutes | Servings 4)

Per serving: 134 Calories; 6.3g Fat; 19.8g Carbs; 2g Protein; 6.9g Sugars

Ingredients

1/2 pound carrots, quartered

1/2 pound parsnip, quartered

1/2 pound pumpkin, cut into small pieces

2 tablespoons butter

2 cloves garlic, crushed

1/2 teaspoon basil

1/2 teaspoon thyme

1/2 teaspoon rosemary

Directions

Add the carrots, parsnips, and pumpkin to the inner pot of your Instant Pot. Pour in 1 cup ofwater.

Secure the lid. Choose the "Manual" mode and cook for 6 minutes at High pressure. Oncecooking is complete, use a quick pressure release; carefully remove the lid.

Drain your vegetables and mash them with a potato masher.

Press the "Sauté" button and melt the butter; the, sauté the aromatics for 1 minute or so. Add thevegetable mash and stir to combine well.

Transfer to a nice serving bowls and garnish with some extra herbs if desired. Bon appétit!

Rice

Wild Rice with Shrimp

(Ready in about 50 minutes | Servings 4)

Per serving: 334 Calories; 8.5g Fat; 36.1g Carbs; 30.9g Protein; 3.1g
Sugars

Ingredients
2 tablespoons olive oil
1 leek, chopped
1 teaspoon garlic, minced
2 bell peppers, chopped
1 cup wild rice
1 cup chicken broth1 rosemary sprig
1 thyme sprig
1 teaspoon kosher salt
1/2 teaspoon ground black pepper
1/2 teaspoon cayenne pepper
1 pound shrimp, deveined
2 tablespoons fresh chives

Directions
Press the "Sauté" button and heat the olive oil. Once hot, sauté the leek
until just tender or about3 minutes.
Then, stir in the garlic and peppers. Continue to cook for 3 minutes
more or until they are tenderand fragrant.
Add the wild rice, broth, and seasonings to the inner pot.
Secure the lid. Choose the "Manual" mode and cook for 30 minutes at
High pressure. Oncecooking is complete, use a natural pressure release
for 10 minutes; carefully remove the lid.
Add the shrimp to the inner pot.
Choose the "Manual" mode and cook for 3 minutes at High pressure.
Once cooking is complete,use a quick pressure release; carefully
remove the lid.
Serve garnished with fresh chives and enjoy!

Late Summer Rice Salad

(Ready in about 30 minutes | Servings 4)

Per serving: 544 Calories; 23.6g Fat; 77.9g Carbs; 6.5g Protein; 14.1g Sugars

Ingredients
1 ½ cups long-grain white rice, rinsed
1 3/4 cups water
1/2 teaspoon table salt
4 tablespoons extra-virgin olive oil
1 tablespoon orange zest
1/4 cup orange juice, freshly squeezed
1 cup grapes, cut in half
1/4 cup dried cranberries
1/2 cup pecans
2 tablespoons pomegranate arils

Directions
Place the rice, water, and salt in the inner pot of your Instant Pot; stir to combine.
Secure the lid. Choose the "Rice" mode and cook for 10 minutes. Once cooking is complete, usea natural pressure release for 15 minutes; carefully remove the lid.
Fluff the rice with a fork and allow it to cool to room temperature.
Add the remaining ingredients to a nice salad bowl; add the chilled rice.
Toss to combine andserve chilled or at room temperature. Bon appétit!

Authentic Paella Valenciana

(Ready in about 25 minutes | Servings 4)

Per serving: 389 Calories; 7.8g Fat; 48.1g Carbs; 31.2g Protein; 2.7g Sugars

Ingredients
2 tablespoons ghee, at room temperature
2 cloves garlic, pressed
1 red bell pepper, cut in strips
1 cup basmati rice
1 pound tiger prawns, deveined
Sea salt and ground black pepper, to taste
1 bay leaf
1 teaspoon paprika
1/4 teaspoon saffron threads
1 tablespoon capers, drained
2 cups chicken broth
1 cup green peas, thawed

Directions
Press the "Sauté" button and melt the ghee. Once hot, cook the garlic and pepper for about 2minutes or until just tender and fragrant.
Add the basmati rice, tiger prawns, salt, black pepper, bay leaf, paprika, saffron, capers, andchicken broth to the inner pot.
Secure the lid. Choose the "Manual" mode and cook for 4 minutes at High pressure. Once cooking is complete, use a natural pressure release for 10 minutes; carefully remove the lid.
Add the green peas to the inner pot; press the "Sauté" button one more time and let it simmeruntil heated through. Enjoy!

Southwestern Rice with Chicken and Beans

(Ready in about 40 minutes | Servings 4)

Per serving: 388 Calories; 4.9g Fat; 53.6g Carbs; 31.6g Protein; 1.8g Sugars

Ingredients
1 cup brown rice
1 cup navy beans, drained and rinsed
1 cup chicken stock
1/2 cup salsa
2 garlic cloves, minced
1 sweet pepper, chopped
1/2 teaspoon cumin
1/2 teaspoon salt
1/2 teaspoon black peppercorns
2 bay leaves
1 pound chicken cutlets

Directions
Place all ingredients in the inner pot. Stir until everything is well combined.
Secure the lid. Choose the "Bean/Chili" mode and cook for 25 minutes at High pressure. Oncecooking is complete, use a natural pressure release for 10 minutes; carefully remove the lid.
Ladle into individual bowls and serve warm. Enjoy!

Eggs & Dairy

Egg Muffins with Ham and Cheese

(Ready in about 15 minutes | Servings 4)

Per serving: 369 Calories; 23.7g Fat; 6.5g Carbs; 31.3g Protein; 1.5g Sugars

Ingredients

8 eggs

1/4 teaspoon ground black pepper, or more to taste

1 teaspoon paprika

Sea salt, to taste

1 cup green peppers, seeded and chopped

8 ounces ham, chopped

1/2 cup sour cream

1/2 cup Swiss cheese, shredded

2 tablespoons parsley, chopped

2 tablespoons cilantro, chopped

2 tablespoons scallions, chopped

Directions

Mix all ingredients until everything is well combined.

Add 1 cup of water and a metal rack to the inner pot of your Instant Pot.

Spoon the prepared mixture into silicone molds. Lower the molds onto the prepared trivet.

Secure the lid. Choose the "Manual" mode and cook for 6 minutes at High pressure. Oncecooking is complete, use a quick pressure release; carefully remove the lid. Bon appétit!

Mexican-Style Omelet with Chanterelles

(Ready in about 30 minutes | Servings 4)

Per serving: 333 Calories; 26.6g Fat; 8.6g Carbs; 16.2g Protein; 3.9g Sugars

Ingredients
1 tablespoon olive oil
1 medium onion, chopped
2 cloves garlic, minced
1 cup Mexica cheese blend, crumbled
1 cup Chanterelle mushrooms, chopped
1 bell pepper, sliced
1 Poblano pepper, seeded and minced
5 eggs
4 ounces cream cheese
Sea salt and ground black pepper, to taste

Directions
Add 1 cup of water and a metal rack to the inner pot of your Instant Pot. Spray a souffle dish andset aside.
Mix all ingredients until well combined. Scrape the mixture into the prepared dish. Lower thesouffle dish onto the rack.
Secure the lid. Choose the "Manual" mode and cook for 11 minutes at High pressure. Oncecooking is complete, use a natural pressure release for 15 minutes; carefully remove the lid.
Serve with salsa if desired. Enjoy!

Italian Frittata with Mushrooms and Spinach

(Ready in about 15 minutes | Servings 4)

Per serving: 335 Calories; 26.5g Fat; 6.5g Carbs; 18.7g Protein; 2.6g Sugars

Ingredients

6 eggs
1/4 cup double cream
1 cup Asiago cheese, shredded
Sea salt and freshly ground black pepper, to taste
1 teaspoon cayenne pepper
2 tablespoons olive oil
1 yellow onion, finely chopped
2 cloves garlic, minced
6 ounces Italian brown mushrooms, sliced
4 cups spinach, torn into pieces
1 tablespoon Italian seasoning mix

Directions

In a mixing bowl, thoroughly combine the eggs, double cream, Asiago cheese, salt, black pepper,and cayenne pepper.
Grease a baking dish with olive oil. Add the remaining ingredients; stir in the egg mixture.Spoon the mixture into the prepared baking dish.
Place 1 cup of water and a metal trivet in the inner pot. Lower the baking dish onto the preparedtrivet.
Secure the lid. Choose the "Manual" mode and cook for 5 minutes at High pressure. Oncecooking is complete, use a quick pressure release; carefully remove the lid. Bon appétit!

Easiest Hard-Boiled Eggs Ever

(Ready in about 15 minutes | Servings 3)

Per serving: 106 Calories; 6.9g Fat; 0.6g Carbs; 9.2g Protein; 0.3g Sugars

Ingredients

5 eggs
1/2 teaspoon salt
1/4 teaspoon red pepper flakes, crushed
2 tablespoons fresh chives, chopped

Directions

Place 1 cup of water and a steamer rack in the inner pot. Arrange the eggs on the rack.

Secure the lid. Choose the "Manual" mode and cook for 5 minutes at High pressure. Oncecooking is complete, use a quick pressure release; carefully remove the lid.

Transfer the eggs to icy-cold water. Now, let them sit in the water bath a few minutes until cool.

Peel your eggs and season with salt and red pepper. Serve garnished with freshly choppedchives. Enjoy!

Snacks & Appetizers

Cheesy Artichoke and Kale Dip

(Ready in about 15 minutes | Servings 8)

Per serving: 190 Calories; 13.2g Fat; 8.3g Carbs; 10.3g Protein; 1g Sugars

Ingredients

12 ounces canned artichoke hearts, chopped

2 cups kale, chopped

1 cup Ricotta cheese

1 ¼ cups Romano cheese, grated

1/2 cup mayonnaise

1 teaspoon gourmet mustard

Salt and ground black pepper, to taste

1 teaspoon garlic powder

1/2 teaspoon shallot powder

1/2 teaspoon cumin powder

Directions

Lightly grease a baking pan that fits inside your Instant Pot. Add all of the above ingredients andstir to combine well.

Add a metal rack to the Instant Pot.

Then, create a foil sling and place it on a rack; lower the baking pan onto the foil strip.

Secure the lid and choose "Manual" function; cook for 9 minutes at High pressure. Once cookingis complete, use a quick release; remove the lid carefully.

Serve with breadsticks on the side. Bon appétit!

Party Dilled Deviled Eggs

(Ready in about 15 minutes + chilling time | Servings 6)

Per serving: 277 Calories; 21.9g Fat; 3.7g Carbs; 15.8g Protein; 1.4g Sugars

Ingredients
10 eggs
1/4 cup extra-virgin olive oil
2 tablespoons mayonnaise
1 teaspoon yellow mustard
tablespoon dill pickle juice
1/2 teaspoon Sriracha sauce
Maldon salt and freshly ground black pepper, to taste
1 tablespoon fresh parsley, chopped
2 tablespoons dill pickle, chopped

Directions
Begin by adding 1 cup of water and a steamer basket to your Instant Pot. Place the eggs in thesteamer basket.
Secure the lid and choose the "Manual" function; cook for 5 minutes at High pressure. Oncecooking is complete, use a natural release; carefully remove the lid.
Slice each egg in half lengthwise.
Transfer the egg yolks to your food processor. Now, add the remaining ingredients; process untilcreamy and smooth.
Then, pipe the chilled filling mixture into the egg whites, overstuffing each. Serve on a niceserving platter and enjoy!

Kid-Friendly Pizza Dip

(Ready in about 25 minutes | Servings 10)

Per serving: 158 Calories; 11.8g Fat; 6.9g Carbs; 5.7g Protein; 3.9g Sugars

Ingredients
10 ounces cream cheese
1 cup tomato sauce
1/2 cup mozzarella cheese, shredded
1/2 cup green olives, pitted and sliced
1/2 teaspoon oregano
1/2 teaspoon basil
1/2 teaspoon garlic salt
1/2 cup Romano cheese, shredded

Directions
Add 1 ½ cups of water and metal trivet to the inner pot. Spritz a souffle dish with cooking spray.

Place the cream cheese on the bottom of the souffle dish. Add the tomato sauce and mozzarellacheese. Scatter sliced olives over the top. Add the oregano, basil, and garlic salt. Top with Romano cheese. Lower the dish onto theprepared trivet.

Secure the lid. Choose the "Manual" mode and cook for 18 minutes at High pressure. Oncecooking is complete, use a quick pressure release; carefully remove the lid.

Serve with chips or breadsticks if desired. Enjoy!

Buttery Carrot Sticks

(Ready in about 10 minutes | Servings 4)

Per serving: 199 Calories; 14.9g Fat; 13.7g Carbs; 4.5g Protein; 6.2g Sugars

Ingredients
1   pound carrots, cut into sticks
1/2 cup dry white wine
1/4 cup water
Sea salt and white pepper, to taste
1/2 stick butter, softened
2   tablespoons agave nectar
1 teaspoon ground allspice
1/2 teaspoon caraway seeds
1 tablespoon fresh lime juice

Directions
Add all of the above ingredients to your Instant Pot.
Secure the lid. Choose the "Manual" mode and High pressure; cook for 2 minutes. Once cookingis complete, use a quick pressure release; carefully remove the lid.
Transfer to a nice serving bowl and enjoy!

Desserts

Double-Chocolate and Peanut Fudge

(Ready in about 15 minutes | Servings 6)

Per serving: 347 Calories; 22.3g Fat; 30.7g Carbs; 5.6g Protein; 21.4g Sugars

Ingredients
8 ounces semisweet chocolate, chopped
2 ounces milk chocolate, chopped
1/3 cup applesauce
1 egg, beaten
1/2 teaspoon vanilla extract
1/2 teaspoon almond extract
1/4 teaspoon ground cinnamon
1/3 cup peanut butter
A pinch of coarse salt
1/4 cup arrowroot powder

Directions
Add 1½ cups of water and a metal trivet to the Instant Pot. Press the "Sauté" button and add thechocolate to a heatproof bowl; melt the chocolate over the simmering water. Press the "Cancel"button.

In a mixing dish, thoroughly combine the applesauce, egg, and vanilla, almond extract,cinnamon, peanut butter and salt.

Then, add the arrowroot powder and mix well to combine. Afterwards, fold in the meltedchocolate; mix again.

Spritz six heat-safe ramekins with a nonstick cooking spray. Pour in the batter and cover withfoil.

Secure the lid. Choose the "Manual" mode and High pressure; cook for 5 minutes. Once cookingis complete, use a quick pressure release; carefully remove the lid.

Let your dessert cool on a wire rack before serving. Bon appétit

Chocolate and Mango Mug Cakes

(Ready in about 15 minutes | Servings 2)

Per serving: 268 Calories; 10.5g Fat; 34.8g Carbs; 10.6g Protein; 31.1g Sugars

Ingredients
1/2 cup coconut flour2 eggs
2 tablespoons honey
1 teaspoon vanilla
1/4 teaspoon grated nutmeg
1 tablespoon cocoa powder
1 medium-sized mango, peeled and diced

Directions
Combine the coconut flour, eggs, honey, vanilla, nutmeg and cocoa powder in two lightlygreased mugs.

Then, add 1 cup of water and a metal trivet to the Instant Pot. Lower the uncovered mugs ontothe trivet.

Secure the lid. Choose the "Manual" mode and High pressure; cook for 10 minutes. Oncecooking is complete, use a quick pressure release; carefully remove the lid.

Top with diced mango and serve chilled. Enjoy!

Old-Fashioned Apple Cake

(Ready in about 1 hour 25 minutes | Servings 8)

Per serving: 304 Calories; 11.8g Fat; 49.7g Carbs; 2.6g Protein; 30.2g Sugars

Ingredients
4 apples, peeled, cored and chopped
1/2 teaspoon ground cloves
1/2 teaspoon ground cardamom
1 teaspoon ground cinnamon
3 tablespoons sugar
1 1/3 cups flour
1 teaspoon baking powder A pinch of salt
1 stick butter, melted
1/2 cup honey
2 tablespoons orange juice
1/2 teaspoon vanilla paste

Directions
Grease and flour a cake pan and set it aside. Toss the apples with the ground cloves, cardamom.cinnamon and sugar.

In a mixing bowl, thoroughly combine the flour, baking powder and salt. In another mixing bowl, mix the butter, honey, orange juice, and vanilla paste. Stir the wetingredients into the dry ones; spoon 1/2 of the batter into the prepared cake pan. Spread half of the apples on top of the batter. Pour in the remaining batter covering the applechunks. Spread the remaining apples on top. Cover the cake pan with a paper towel. Add 1 cup of water and a metal rack to your Instant Pot. Lower the cake pan onto the rack. Secure the lid. Choose the "Manual" mode and cook for 55 minutes at High pressure. Oncecooking is complete, use a natural pressure release for 10 minutes; carefully remove the lid. Transfer the cake to a cooling rack and allow it to sit for about 15 minutes before slicing and serving.

Classic Chewy Brownies

(Ready in about 40 minutes | Servings 12)

Per serving: 264 Calories; 18.1g Fat; 24.2g Carbs; 4.5g Protein; 19.3g Sugars

Ingredients
1/2 cup walnut butter
1/2 cup sunflower seed butter
1 cup coconut sugar
1/2 cup cocoa powder
2 eggs
A pinch of grated nutmeg
A pinch of salt
1/2 cardamom powder
1/2 teaspoon cinnamon powder
1/2 teaspoon baking soda
1 teaspoon vanilla extract
1/2 cup dark chocolate, cut into chunks

Directions
Place a metal trivet and 1 cup of water in your Instant Pot. Spritz a baking pan with nonstickcooking spray.

In a mixing bowl, combine all ingredients, except for the chocolate; stir well to create a thickbatter.

Spoon the batter into the prepared pan. Sprinkle the chocolate chunks over the top; gently pressthe chocolate chunks into the batter.

Lower the baking pan onto the trivet.

Secure the lid. Choose the "Manual" mode and cook for 20 minutes at High pressure. Oncecooking is complete, use a natural pressure release for 10 minutes; carefully remove the lid.

Place your brownies on a cooling rack before slicing and serving. Bon appétit!

CPSIA information can be obtained
at www.ICGtesting.com
Printed in the USA
LVHW051654010621
689062LV00009B/558

9 781802 751451